Step by Step Guide how to Buy, Store and Trade with Bitcoin & Altcoins

Preface

The book 'Step by Step Guide how to Buy, Store and Trade with Bitcoin & Altcoins' was created by my passion for cryptocurrency. The last year I changed my opinion for Bitcoins from a forbidden/illegal area for me to a risky but full of potential opportunities project. It is the first book I have written in my life, so please forgive me for the spelling mistakes or syntax errors as I am not a native English speaker. In this book I will try to provide practical information with examples how to buy bitcoins & altcoins, store them (hot and cold wallets) and identify opportunities between the 500+ coins and tokens in the market.

I would like to state two things to my readers: a) I am not a financial advisor and all the information I will provide to you are coming from my personal research and the knowledge I have accumulated the last year. I will focus on platforms such as Coibase, Kraken and Bittrex. I am not going to include any paid link as I am not interested for affiliate marketing. I am using these platforms as I am happy with the quality of services and reputation. Some readers could state that Poloniex or Bitfinex or BitFlyer or Bithumb are much better and we can have more options. Actually I am happy to accept your feedback and improve the level of my knowledge. So the first lesson is to be open to suggestions and recommendations and please feel free to send an email to tutor4bitcoin@gmail.com. b) From the other hand a significant percent of people who are investing in bitcoin and especial in altcoins are expecting to be rich with small capital and short amount of time. We have seen in the news that people invest in the early days of bitcoin and now they are millioners. It is a good fairy tale who happened to a few people, but the truth is that is not the case anymore. Don't get me wrong. They are tremendous opportunities out there and potential for significant wealth, but you need to have a strategy and a long term plan. Some readers of the book will remember the 'dot com' bubble, where people lost their fortunes, because they bought stocks in companies which had only a webpage. History has its tendency to repeat itself. I hope through my book I can help you to develop a long term strategy.

Thank you again for purchasing my book. If you need private SKYPE lessons, please email me to tutor4bitcoin@gmail.com and we can arrange a 2h lesson where we can discuss advanced tools for trading and the altcoin market (for my readers I will provide a special price of $29.99 from $49.99). I try to become a best person, writer, investor so please feel free to leave a feedback to Amazon reviews. Thank you again and welcome to the cryptocurrency market.

Author: Emmanouil Paraskevas

Step by Step Guide how to Buy, Store and Trade with Bitcoin & Altcoins

Contents

Chapter 1: Why everyone is talking about Bitcoin?...3

Chapter 2: Buy, Store and Trade Bitcoin & Altcoins...6

    2.1 Coinbase platform...6

    2.2 Kraken platform...9

    2.3 Buy altcoins with Bittrex plaform...14

Chapter 3: How to spot opportunities?..20

Chapter 4: Blockchain and Mining..24

Chapter 5: Epilogue..26

Author: Emmanouil Paraskevas

Chapter 1: Why everyone is talking about Bitcoin?

I am quite sure that you heard in the news that some hackers attacked a few hundred thousand computers across the world and for ransom, they wanted to get paid by bitcoins. Also in the dark web, illicit transactions are completed through bitcoins. But my favorite part is when you hear in the news that someone invested a few thousand dollars and now he is a millionaire. Actually that is true, because if someone invested €100 or $100 (apologies for the graphs as some are in Euro and some are in Dollar) in January 2013 he or she would probably have now around €40k value in bitcoins (The price on 6th January 2013 was around €10 and on 11th October 2017 the price was almost €4,028. Price trends can be seen on Picture 1 and taken by the Coinbase webpage).

Picture 1: Price trend of bitcoin from January 2013 until October 2017 (source: www.Coinbase.com)

With the current price of Bitcoin an investor with €100 can afford to buy a few million Satoshi. 1 Bitcoin or the symbol BTC as you can see in the exchange platforms is equal with 100 million Satoshi. Please keep this information as couple of trading platforms provide exchange rate with dollar, euro, yen, rubble or with bitcoin. When you open an account with trading platforms, they will ask you to confirm your account/address/bank account. Until the confirmation is completed, you can trade altcoins with bitcoin and not with fiat currency which is dollar, euro,….

Let me give some interesting but boring overview why bitcoin is interesting. Satoshi Nakamoto (nobody knows his identity, if he is real or it is a team of people) published a paper in October 2008 and he set up the foundations of bitcoin. In summary when you buy a bitcoin, you have accepted that digital money has a value for you. We trust dollar, euro, or yen because we know that it is used by strong countries (political, financial, military), which are back up by central banks and regulatory institutes. Please forget these topics for bitcoins and altcoins. When I read this information, I said to myself: Why I need to trust bitcoin? The answer is the same way I am trusting dollar, euro, yen or any other fiat currency. Dollar has a value for you as you can exchange fiat money with products or services. That is the way you learned by your parents, grandparents, uncles, aunts…..

We are not living in our grandparents time as internet has changed everything the last 20 years. We can order food from online groceries, book our flight tickets with our credit card, buy a used car from Ebay, a laptop from Amazon (apologies for Ebay and Amazon funs as they are some interesting videos in Youtube of which platform is the best for each topic), invest in bonds or have real money in our bank accounts. Actually since '70, when we left the 'the rule of gold', the printed money represents only 5% of the total money which are in circulation in daily basis. So why our economy does not fall down? Because we are happy to have our money in the bank for 0.05% interest rate (so we are losing money as the inflation is higher than the interest rate), but the financial institute can invest them and make more money based on our hard labor.

When you buy bitcoin, you are accepting the cryptocurrency philosophy, which can be summarized below:

1. **No borders**: For the first time in human history we are having a global accepted currency (even a digital one which you will never hold it in your hand or maybe with a cold wallet), which can be transferred from one account to another in any country much faster than traditional banking transactions (actually there is a debate here as bitcoin transactions are faster in comparison with traditional institutes transactions, but as more transactions added into the blockchain it will take more time. Don't worry as startup companies pop up like mushrooms and they are promising new generation of coins or processes based on the blockchain which can solve our problems and improve our life related with the financial, insurance, banking, supply chain and many more sectors.
2. **Anonymity**: That is an interesting part as the transactions are posted in the blockchain but nobody knows which person/company was behind (of course if they want to find and dig more, they can find your IP and found your details especial if it is the IRS. Actually they are altcoins which are promising improved anonymity in comparison with bitcoin and it could be a good area for study in the near future).
3. **No control by central authority**: As I explained before bitcoin is not backed up by central authorities, which means they cannot decide to undervalue or overvalue this coin according to their will. Also there is a specific number of bitcoins which can be created through mining (there is a cap of 21 million) and that means it is not affected by inflation. The value of your Bitcoins will increase in the future and that sounds a logical investment (actual there is the argument because if Central Authorities in different countries forbid their citizens to hold and trade bitcoins, its value will reach the bottom).
4. **Security**: My favorite part. Time to time you read in the news that hackers attacked a company and stole bitcoins. People lost their money, because they were not secured (not accepted currency and not stored in state approved financial institute). All of these are creating bad reputation and hesitation. If you study the hacking incidents, everyone can understand that the process which is creating bitcoins was not affected but the companies which stored the bitcoin were hacked (if you have free time, please feel free to google the MtGox incident and why so much money get lost). Bitcoin is based on the Blockchain which means that there is a global

network of computers, which are confirming the transactions. You can lose your bitcoin if your share your private wallet details or store them in an untrusted company, but hackers cannot amend the blockchain and steal your money (actually it can be done in theoretical level. They need to copy the network which is processing bitcoins and if at least 51% of network confirm their hacked transactions, they can steal your money. That is really really really difficult for bitcoin as the resources they need to devoted and spent are extremely high).

Chapter 2: Buy, Store and Trade Bitcoin & Altcoins

Hopefully you did not regret that you spent your money for nothing on this book as Chapter 1 was too theoretical. I believe it gave you a generic overview of the cryptocurrency philosophy and it has put the foundation stones for your investing strategy. Before we jump buying Bitcoins & Altcoins, we need to understand the driving force of cryptocurrencies. The investment strategy is a combination of knowledge for the product (in that case bitcoin & altcoins), financial data (graphs, evaluation, forecast) and taking the risk (important note: Always invest as much money as you can afford to lose. In my case I have a portfolio of €500 and I am increasing it by 20% in monthly basis. If I lose my money today, I am going to be sad but I knew the risk. That is the reason I have the best case and worst case scenario in each transaction. For worst case scenario I accept losses 10 to 20% of my capital, before I decide to withdraw. In any case I cannot lose more than 20%).

Now the exciting part. How to buy bitcoins. They are actually dozens of webpages who can offer you bitcoins in different exchanges and different fiat currencies. My advice is when you do the first transaction, add a small amount of money, buy bitcoins and then take and store them to your personal wallet. Actually these companies are providing storage for your coins or 'hot wallets'. Of course there is a risk as they can be hacked and you can lose your bitcoins. In my case I started with Coinbase and I have to admit it is a simple and easy to use webpage. Actually every book I read and a few crypto news webpages recommended it and I had good experience so far (with the exception of my ID conformation as I tried to scan my passport through the webcamera of my laptop and it failed a few times. I sent them an email and after a couple days they confirmed my account). Coinbase is available for 33 countries the last time I looked their webpage, so please check if you can deposit your own fiat currency to start trading.

2.1 Coinbase platform

As you can see from Picture 2 you can buy, sell or send to different accounts only 3 cryptocoins (Bitcoin, Ethereum and Litecoin). These are three of the most popular coins with market value above $1 billion, good reputation, good engineering team and good supporting community.

https://www.coinbase.com/dashboard

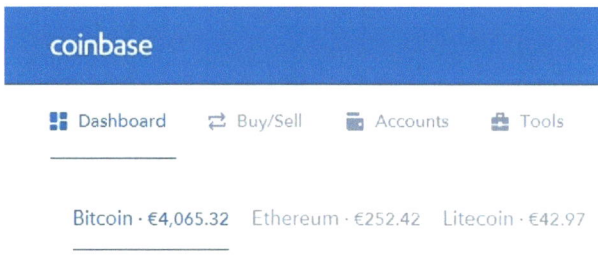

Picture 2: A screenshot from Coinbase webpage

Step by Step Guide how to Buy, Store and Trade with Bitcoin & Altcoins

It is a really simple webpage, but if you have questions email me or we can set up a private skype lesson of how you can set up your account, but believe me it is a simple process (if you don't have any issues with scanning your passport).

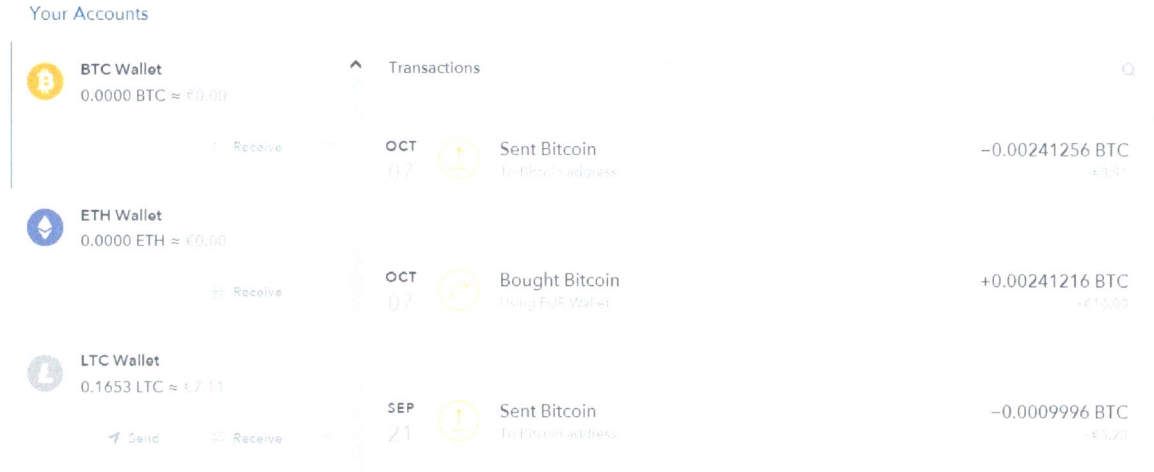

Picture 3: Overview of my accounts in Coinbase

When you press the tab 'Accounts', you can see how much bitcoin, ethereum and litecoin you have in your accounts (this is a training account and for that reason the value is very small). As you can see I own only 0.1653 Litecoin, which the total value is €7.11 (market value on 11th October). Same logic for the rest of the coins.

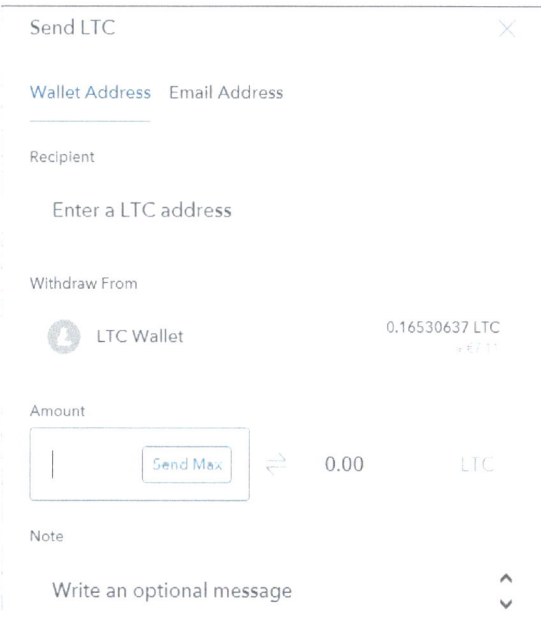

Picture 4: Send option for Litecoin

Author: Emmanouil Paraskevas

The most important part is the address of the recipient. My Litecoin address can be found below as an example (of course I don't want to use my own address as I will be charged to send my own money to my wallet again). So you need to copy the 34 letters (it varies from coin to coin) and paste it on the LTC address. I have a few applications on my mobile phone where you can scan the QR code and automatically you have the address (I have a few crypto wallets from Freewallets and I downloaded them from Google play. Personally I am very happy with the apps but I read a feedback I did not like, so I have limited amount of coins there. Copay app is really good, as it offers you also the opportunity to exchange bitcoins with Amazon gift cards. Amazon does not accept for now direct bitcoins and it is a good indirect way to exchange bitcoins with products. It is only applicable for Amazon USA).

Picture 5: Litecoin address in Coinbase

After that the process is simple, as you enter the amount of money in Litecoin you want to send. You need to pay the network fee and then you press continue and confirm the transaction. Same logic for Bitcoin and Ethereum and you can use Coinbase as your hot wallet.

2.2 Kraken platform

I heard for the first time the name Kraken when I was 15 years old when I saw the movie 'Clash of the Titans' (the classical version). Maybe it is a mistake and I made a spelling mistake, but I have to admit it is a catchy title.

Sail the high seas of success.

BUY, SELL, & TRADE BITCOIN

CREATE AN ACCOUNT

Picture 6: Snapshot for Kraken trading platform

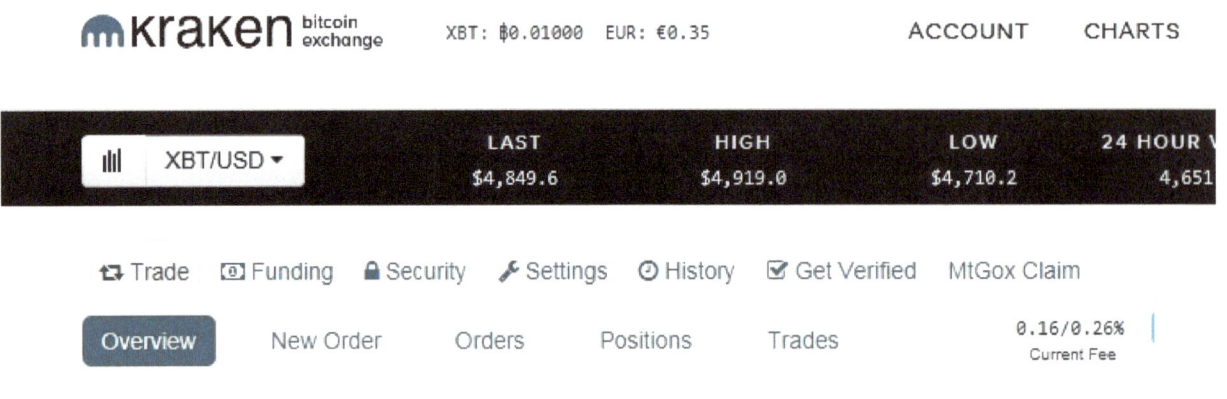

Picture 7: Overview for Kraken trading platform

Really simple platform and straightforward. I really like also the customer services as I had to change my personal details and their support was really good, fast and polite. Before you start the trading, you need to verify your account, personal details, address and ID. That will permit you to change level and you can trade from cryptocurrencies only (Tier 1) up to $200,000 in monthly basis (Tier 4). It is legal obligation to confirm your ID and the rest of technical information. It will take some time, but it worth from my perspective.

Picture 7: Available options of cryptocurrencies on Kraken trading platform

Of course they are other platforms in which some readers have more experience and as I have stated to my introduction I am open to suggestions. With Kraken you can buy, sell or exchange around 20 cryptocurrencies, which are popular among investors. It offers you the opportunity to deposit money in Euro, Dollar and Yen, but you need to have at least Tier 2 level confirmation. If you have any issues email me or ask technical support. They are really good and fast.

Step by Step Guide how to Buy, Store and Trade with Bitcoin & Altcoins

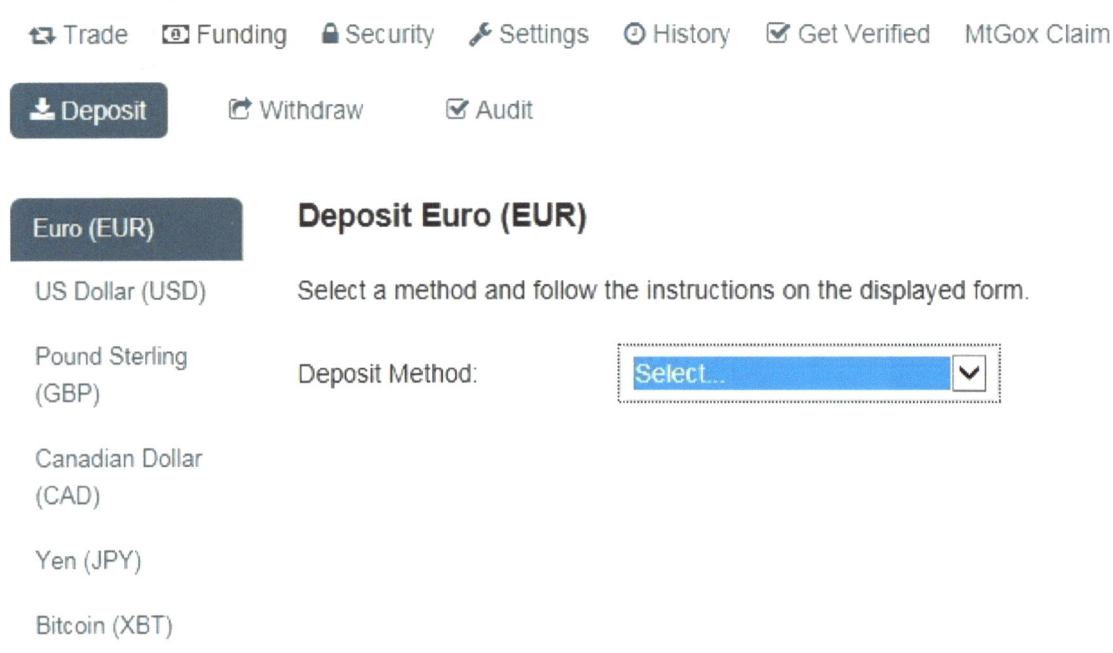

Picture 8: Deposit Euro funds on Kraken trading platform

Simple process where you select the option to Deposit funds, choose your currency and then select the deposit method. They will provide you their banking details and you will log in to your account and send the amount of money you need to invest (first time start with a small amount to confirm your account in Kraken and then feel free to increase the limit based on your budget).

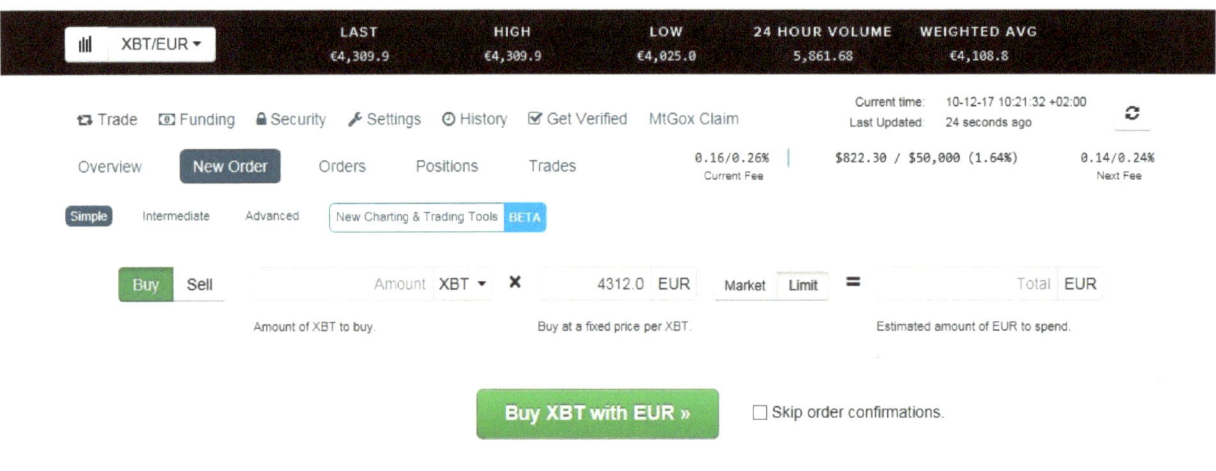

Picture 9: Buy Bitcoin on Kraken trading platform

Author: Emmanouil Paraskevas

I have to admit that I was excited the first time I bought bitcoin, but disappointed after 2 min as I bought only 0.1 BTC or 10,000,000 Satoshi. The process was simple. The option 'Buy' was selected (Green color button) and you can see the current price of Bitcoin in € of $ (depends of your currency you have selected). You have 2 options: Market and Limit. If you press the button Market, you will buy in the current market price. If you press Limit, you can select the price you want to buy. It all depends if you want to wait for the price to go down (from the Technical Analysis you will learn in Chapter 4) or you want to own BTC as soon as possible.

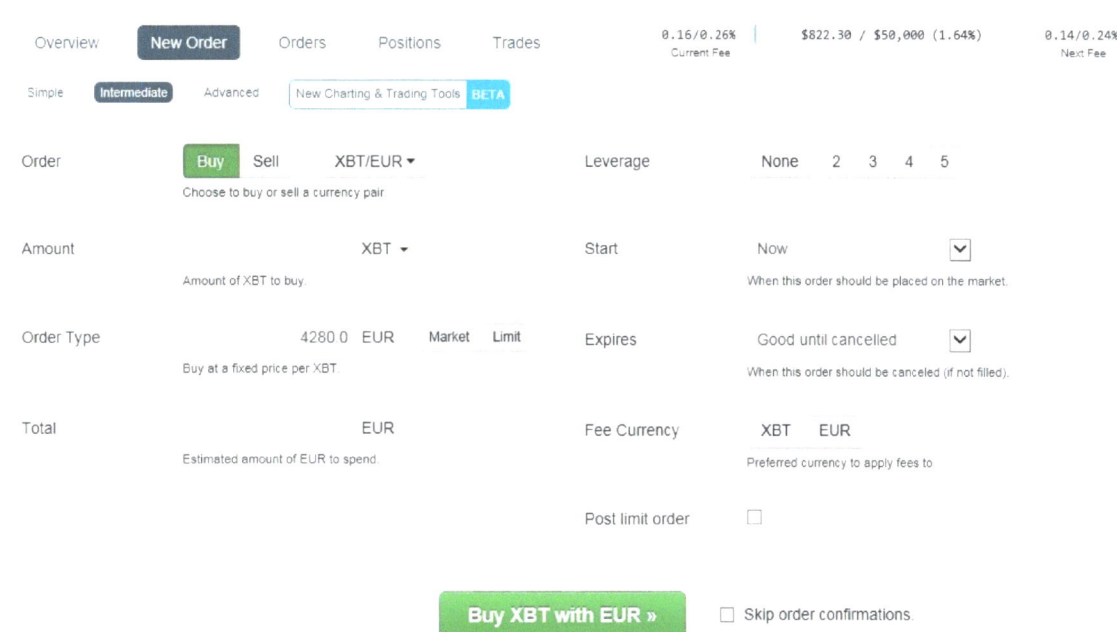

Picture 10: Advanced options to buy Bitcoin on Kraken trading platform

Kraken is a trading platform and it can offer you leverage. That is a tricky part and you need to have experience and training in trading, because having leverage for example 5 you can borrow up to 5 times the money you want to invest. For example I want to buy 5 BTC and I have 1 BTC only. I use leverage 5 and I got the rest from Kraken (not for free). You need to return them back and if you do some investments (for example you bought a different coin which you bet that it will go up and bitcoin down) which were not effective, then you need to return 4 BTC or €16k back to Kraken. I am not a financial advisor, but if you decide to use leverage please consider the entry and exit strategy in each case.

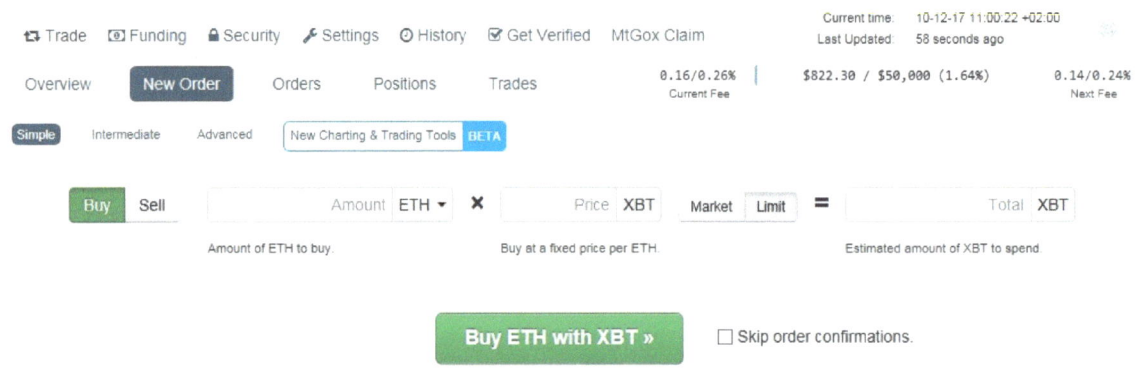

Picture 11: Buy Ethereum with Bitcoin on Kraken trading platform

Same logic you bought Bitcoin with Dollar or Euro, you can buy other altcoins using Bitcoin for example Ethereum (ETH. Don't be confused with ETC which is Ethereum Classic as they were splitted a couple of months ago due a hacking instance. The ETH is using the new updated safe protocol, but some members of the Ethereum stayed to the old protocol as they think it is better). Similar story with Bitcoin and Bitcoin cash, as again some members of Bitcoin community changed the protocol to make it faster and created the Bitcoin cash. Bitcoin will update also its protocol soon and it could affect positively or negatively the price of Bitcoin cash (so far Bitcoin cash is going well, but nobody can predict the future).

2.3 Buy altcoins with Bittrex plaform

Now we are at the point, where you are going to ask yourself: how am I going to make money as I don't have high budget or I heard from a friend of mine who bought a coin and he got 1,000% back of his investment? Apologies if I sound boring, but I am not going to give and I don't want to give these kind of information. I am not a financial advisor, the cryptocurrency market is relative new and risky and they are some 'whales' out there. I don't know the history of the term 'whales' (maybe it is based on the fact that it is the biggest animal on earth and with its weight it can flush you very easy with its tail or the contrast of 'sharks' for Wall Street), but I understand that they are people or organizations with significant sum of money which can increase and decrease the price of the coin (usually with a market cap between $ 1 to 20 million), based on their will.

When we see a price of the coin goes up, it is part of the human psychology to follow and buy it, because it is an opportunity. But when we see the price goes down, we panic and sell with losses. So you need to establish the investment strategy with the following oath:

1. I …..(your name) should not be excited and follow the wave to buy coins which are going up and down like a roller coster
2. I …..(your name) should not panic and sell my portfolio, because the prices went down and it is not aligned with my investment strategy and in/out policy
3. I …….(your name) should do my homework and study each coin I want to buy/sell

4. I ….. (your name) will not invest more money than I cannot afford to lose
5. I…..(your name) want to play the long term game and help my crypto brothers and sisters in the battlefield of crypto war

Now you feel optimistic as it is going to be a very excited game with sadness and joys, but above all with losers and winners. The fact that you are reading this book, you are already in the winning side as you spent money to buy a book for the cryptocurrencies.

A summary of points you need to consider when you want to invest in alt coins:

- **Company who is creating the coin** (they are companies which are promising a novel solution to our problems using Blockchain technology. They offer ICO = Initial Coin Offering, where you can buy coins with a discount. These companies will solve our problems in education, supply chain, financial but for their transactions you need to use their offered tokens. They are interesting articles in google where they claim that tokens are better than coins. Coins can do one thing: to be used for payment. With tokens we can do more than that: smart contracts, payments, monitoring….hundreds of attributes based on the skills of the company)
- **Engineering team and support** (they are some early investors in bitcoin who are looking to expand their funds in new opportunities. They are helping startup companies with their expertise and brand name to build the strategy of the company)
- **Market/Problem/Technology** (each company is doing a market analysis to identify the biggest piece of the pie which can take with their coin/token. To find a market is a good starting point, but to overpromising for example a coin which can be used for everything is not a good advertisement. They need to have an established technology or develop a realistic technology to solve the problem for the specific market in the near future)
- **Market cap** (a very good webpage is https://coinmarketcap.com/ where you can find all coins, the top 100 per day, prices and total market volume in $. You can see the trend of the price during time and visit the webpage of each coin).
- **Media cover** (More and more startup companies are securing funds of couple of million dollars and they attract the interest of special financial news webpages and blogs. That is a good starting point for your research)
- **Supporting community** (I put it last but actually it is one of the most important parameters you need to consider during your strategy development. If there is not a strong community who is backing up the coin, that means that people are not interested to use it)

In that point, I know you ask to yourself 'This guy is talking a lot and he does not give us any tip which coin we need to buy'. As I promised I won't do, but I was in the same position like you when I was reading all the books in the market. So for that reason I would like to show you my strategy in crypto investment. I have 2 portfolios with the names: 1. The Mountain portfolio 2. The Wind portfolio.

In my Mountain portfolio as the name suggests it is my stable selection of cryptocurrencies (taking in consideration that the market is votile and risky). I have put 67% of my capital and it consists of the following coins:

Table 1: Mountain portfolio

Cryptocurrency	Percent in the Portfolio
Bitcoin	25%
Ethereum	35%
Ripple	35%
Litcoin	5%

In my Wind portfolio I have accepted high risk (to a risky market) and I have allocated only 33% of my capital. I have accepted losses of 10-20% before I withdraw partial my funds from my portfolio, but I am really happy and confidence to keep all the coins for the next 1 to 2 years.

Table 2: Wind portfolio

Cryptocurrency	Percent in the Portfolio
Monero	20%
Arc	20%
Siacoin	20%
Neo	15%
OmiseGo	15%
Lisk	10%

Very soon I will create different portfolios which I am going to categorize based on the solution they provide for example cloud solutions, web solutions, financial solutions etc. If you want to learn more, send me an email and we can set up a SKYPE private lesson of how you can find the ideal portfolio, based on your needs.

Hopefully you are happy with the information I gave you, but please don't copy my selections and tomorrow come back and say 'I lost money because of you'. I am not a financial advisor and that is my portfolio based on my research and selections. I can always amend it, but for now I am happy with my choices. Now the logical question is where I can buy coins such as Neo (I love and hate Neo coin. It can be a new Ethereum, but it is developed in China. There is huge uncertainty if China will embrace or reject

Step by Step Guide how to Buy, Store and Trade with Bitcoin & Altcoins

cryptocurrencies. As a concept Neo is interesting and hopefully I will improve my position to this coin). Please do your own research but for coins that I cannot find on Coinbase or Kraken, I go to Bittrex.com (https://bittrex.com/Home/Markets).

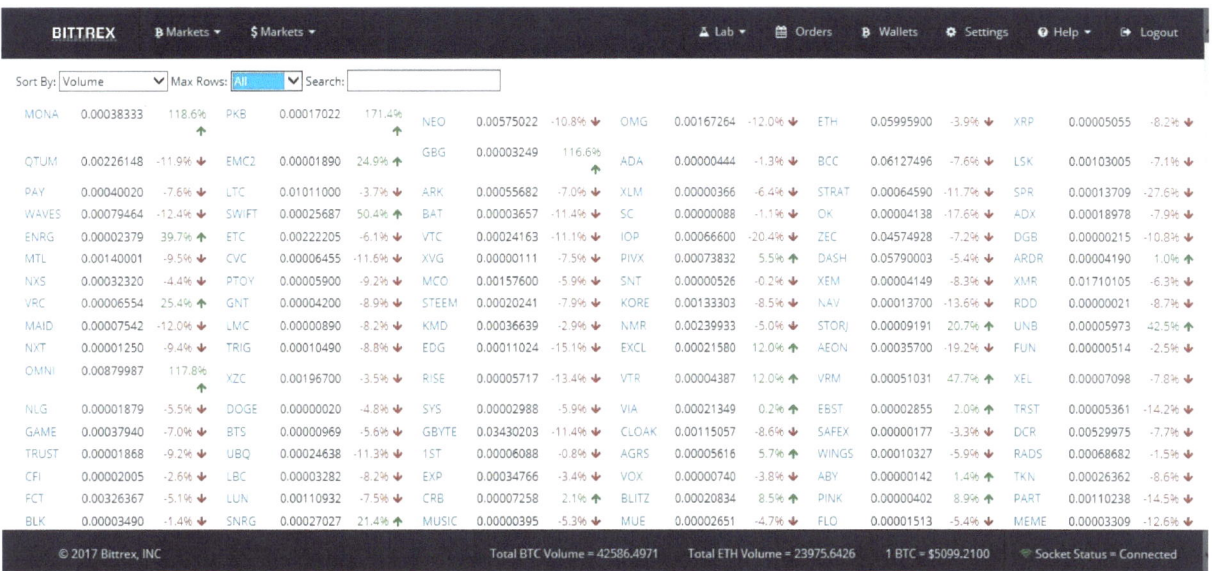

Picture 12: Overview of altcoins on Bittrex platform

I love Bittrex. Initially I was confused but I realized it is really simple. I have the basic account with this platform and I can deal 3 BTC volume per day. I top up my account with Bitcoins and I can buy my selected coins.

Picture 13: Main Menu on Bittrex platform

Select Wallets and then Bitcoin. Press the cross or plus symbol (+) and you can see the bitcoin address for this platform. With minus symbol (-) you can withdraw your funds to your wallet.

Picture 14: Top up or Witdraw Bitcoins on Bittrex platform

Author: Emmanouil Paraskevas

Step by Step Guide how to Buy, Store and Trade with Bitcoin & Altcoins

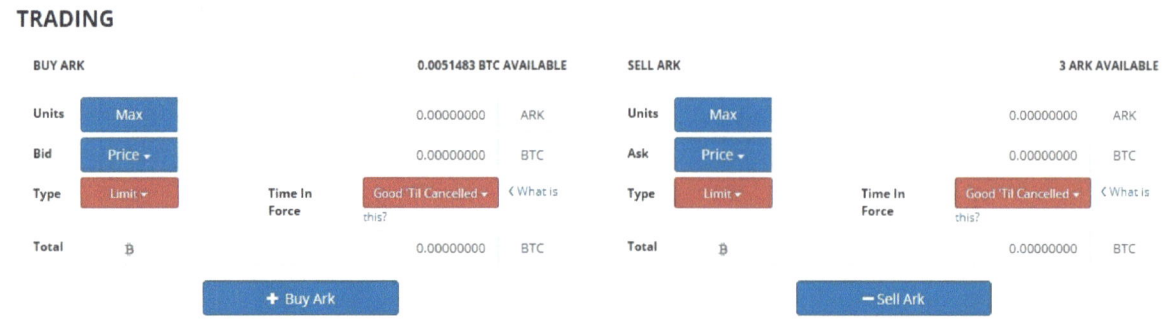

Picture 15: Trading options for Arc coin on Bittrex platform

You can find Arc from the main menu (from the Dollar market or Bitcoin market) and you can select if you want to buy or select. In this training account, I can select how much Arc coins I want based on the available capital (to be honest sometimes I am bored to calculate the Satoshi to Dollar and then see how much I want. Usually I press max (the Blue button in both cases Buy and Sell) and I see how much coins I can buy or sell. Then I decide if I like the market price or place a bid (same logic with the Kraken platform). If you are happy with the settings, I place and confirm the order. If you have any questions, you know the process (email or ask for a private SKYPE lesson). Read also the history of the team and it seems that they appreciate security and I am happy to keep my funds also there (you receive email all the time when you try to log in. If you have a different IP, you need to confirm it through your email account. Once I was in a hotel and I tried seven times before i finally log in to my Bittrex account. I love it and hate it, as I felt safe but also said: I lost my funds. You can always log in from your home IP and you can increase the security settings with an Authedicator app).

I did not want to write more for this topic as I want to keep some information for my students plus you probably want to delete this book if it is overloaded. I just want to give you some 'food for thought' topics:

a) https://www.cryptopia.co.nz/Exchange/?baseMarket=BTC: If you are not happy with all the platforms and you want something risky and potential high value, use cryptopia. You can find coins/tokens, which you never heard in your life. I have not used it so far but it is my target for the next 4 weeks. Send me an email and I will provide my review from my blog
b) https://www.blockchain.com/: I want to be honest with you. That is my main hot wallet for long term storage. Actually you create your own bank as you have a unique ID, nobody knows how much funds you have except you, you have a private and public key and you can log in from any place across the world (with challenges but that is good)
c) https://localbitcoins.com/: From the feedback and the forums I have been, it is a recommendation as it is considered cheaper and better in comparison with the previous platforms I have mentioned. Again I need to evaluate and I will provide feedback to my blog

d) https://electrum.org/#home: Good recommendation from forums for offline wallets. Actually I have the portable version, my private keys and a usb stick. So my stick is my wallet (actually I don't recommend it to people as the portable version was not opening to my laptop and I said 'ops!!! I lost my funds'. I restarted my laptop and problem was solved but please don't try to be in the same position as I was. Not a pleasant experience and it is not recommended by Electrum)

e) https://www.myetherwallet.com/: I bought some tokens from a startup company and I gave them my ether wallet address. Most of the ether wallets I used so far, does not support other tokens in Ethereum network. I did not use address from exchange platforms such as Kraken, but I lost the tokens. The company recommended since Day 1 to use mytherwallet webpage. I did not hear them and I lost my money. Painful lesson: Listen to the company's recommendation and know which coin you want to buy

f) https://trezor.io/: For people who do not trust hot-online wallets. They are some companies in the market such as trezor where you can store your cryptocoin offline, and access them through a special software and passwords. These are the cold wallets.

Chapter 3: How to spot opportunities?

That is the $ 1 million question. The short answer is to go to a person who can predict the future. But in that case why you don't ask him/her for the lottery ticket number. It will be faster and probably you will earn more money.

The long answer is through the study of the market, reading books, listening/giving/taking opinions, investing, making mistakes, watching Youtube videos for this topic, going to seminars, taking risks and designing a long term strategy. Believe me I really hate that, as I am not a book reader but there is motivation. After a while it is funny and if you like Math and you have invested in stocks in the past, the principles are similar. I will try to give an overview of technical analysis and if you need more information, I am available (apologies as this book is also a promotion of my hobby as a tutor. I used to help teenagers in my free time to pass their summer exams in Chemistry, Physic, Math and I know how desperate my students were until I gave them the SOS questions, so they could get the pass score).

Please find below some example of Technical analysis using $:BTC ratio as a case study from Bittrex graphs. Of course every technical analysis should be supported by analysis of market, company who sells the coin or external factors such as regulatory affairs (my opinion and please keep it or leave it: even if China or Russia or EU or USA say that bitcoin is forbidden and the price goes down to $100, I will still keep my Satoshi and I will buy more BTC because countries such as Switzerland, Taiwan, Japan, Thailand... support and embrace bitcoins and cryptocurrencies. The revolution started and it will have long term effects to our life. Same way as internet has changed our life a generation ago, cryptocurrencies will do the same).

a) Bollinger bands

My favorite tool as I can see the range of prices, which are logical for bitcoin. There is a rally again and in my case I am waiting to have a correction and then I will buy again BTC. The clear trend analysis to the top means that people are following the wave. History shows that they will be scared and sell when the price goes down.

Step by Step Guide how to Buy, Store and Trade with Bitcoin & Altcoins

b) MACD (Moving Average Convergence Divergence)

Please look the two lines below, the grey and red. The grey is above the red and that is an indicator that investors are buying BTC. From the other hand I see the volumes (the small red/green bar under the candles symbols). The volume are not that high, which means that big investors are not buying now. Very logical as the follow the moto 'buy low, sell high'. They are waiting the price to fall down and then they will buy.

Author: Emmanouil Paraskevas

c) RSI (Relative Strength Index)

With RSI index you can see if the BTC is overbought (upper limit) or oversold (lower limit). Watching the grey line you can see that BTC price is at the limit of overbought and soon a correction will follow. Then there will be an opportunity for investing.

Chapter 4: Blockchain and Mining

Before I answer the question 'Is mining worth the investment?', I would like to explain with my own worlds what is mining. As we leaned hopefully from Chapter 1, Bitcoin is a decentralized cryptocurrency which nobody has ownership of its identity. When you buy Bitcoin or send BTC to a specific address you trust the Blockchain process that nobody will steal your money during the transfer. Also it secures that you don't lie also to your customers or companies who collaborate with you. For example you want to buy a pair of shoes from 5 online retailers who accept BTC for payments. You can order at the same time 5 pairs of shoes and pay them once (with the same BTC). If it was not for the Blockchain to assure the traceability process for each transaction, verify the first payment and raise the red flag for the rest of the payments, you could go away with 5 pairs at 20% of the initial cost for each one.

So miners, the people or institutes who contribute their computer capacity to the network to confirm all this transactions in the Blockchain for Bitcoin are needed. Without them, the Bitcoin cannot succeed and as more people/investors start to use Bitcoin, more and more transactions need to be verified in daily basis. That is the reason there is a fee when you conduct a transaction, so computers should pay the expenses and contribute their capacity to the network. The good old days which I missed them, the miners used to mine dozens of BTC as the mathematical complexity to solve the problems/confirm transactions were relative easy (of course the price for 1 BTC was a few dollars). Also you could have mined with your normal laptop (actually there is a story in the newspaper for a guy who lost his laptop and he had a few thousand BTC on it. He was looking in the waste area of his city to find his laptop and he started a fund raising event for this topic). That is not the case anymore as we need to spend a significant amount of money to buy special graphic cards, which are developed for mining (you can find online different options from $500 to $2,500). Then you need to calculate how much money you need to spend for electricity (the mining process is very energy intensive), maintenance, upgrade, protection from hackers, shutdowns, technical skills, manpower, noise etc. Even then you need to consider to join a pool where you contribute your capacity power with other members of the team and then analogically you split the profits (as much power you have as much faster you can solve the problems in comparison with the competition in the network and take the reward, which is coming from the fee we pay for each transaction). Personally I don't feel optimistic to invest on bitcoin mining, but I have a friend who thinks it worth based on the online calculators he has used (they are dozens available on google. If he was based in China or in a country with cheap electricity, yes it worth the investment). From the other hand i don't have the same opinion for other type of coin mining and especial for the 'silver' of cryptocoins, which is Litecoin. You can still mine with your normal laptop and you can make a profit. Plus you mine Litcoins which can get significant increase on its value the next 1 to 2 years.

My personal experience with mining was with Genesis mining or cloud mining. I was lucky as I bought a contract without expire day, but with minimum processing capacity. From my contract I am receiving the BTC from the fee which my capacity has helped to process the bitcoin transactions (minus the daily maintenance fee). In the first year it will give me back 100% ROI. When I was happy and comfortable to upgrade my contract, they were out of contracts. With the publicity of bitcoins they manage to increase their customers from 500,000 to 1,000,000 and now they have a few contacts left for less known coins. Of course this case can change in the future for example upgrade their total capacity and offer new contracts. I tried also with hasling24.com, but they were also run out of contracts. In October 2017 they announced increase of capacity but they offer 3 years contract (instead of unlimited time) and increased price in comparison with the unlimited contract. They are a few dozen companies across the world who offer cloud mining, but there is a risk of scam. Please review them, look for a feedback from previous customers and then decide to invest or not. Actually I have read a few negative comments for Genesis mining also, but personally they have provided good level of services so far to me (the customer support replied to me after 2 days and I receive my BTC to my wallet every 45 days. Some people bought a better contract and receive BTC in daily basis. It all depends from the capacity. Higher capacity means more problems solved and more rewards).

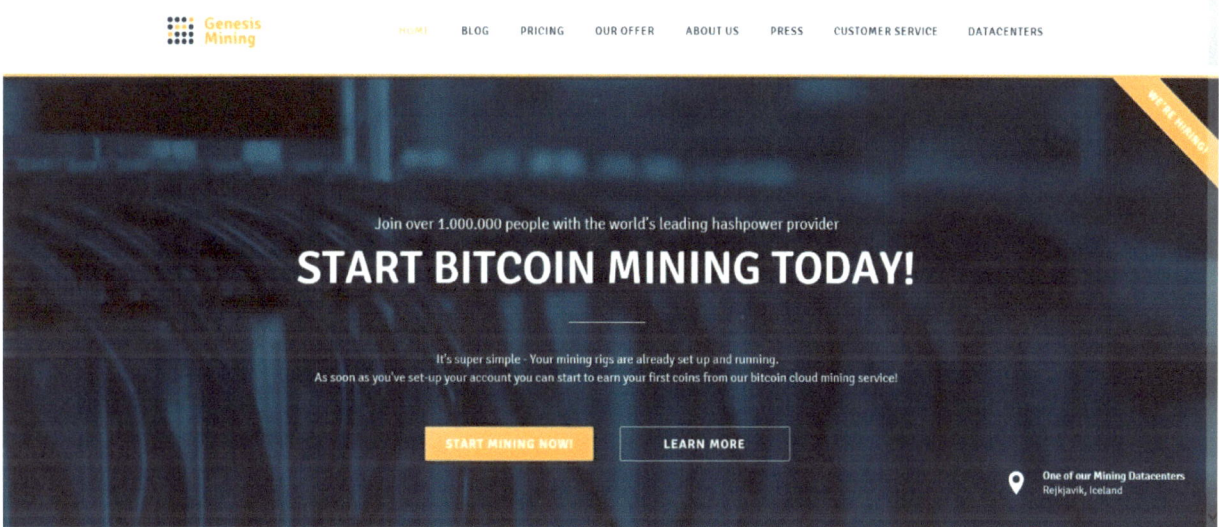

Picture 16: Cloud mining with Genesis Mining platform

Chapter 5: Epilogue

Thank you for your patience so far. Every day I am trying to learn something new and if I made any mistake or did not clarify a topic as much as I should, please email me with your comments. I would appreciate if you leave me a feedback to Amazon and hopefully you will give me a motivation to write the second part of my book, which will have the title 'Advanced techniques for Technical Analysis and Diversification of Cryptocoins Portfolio'.

If you want to take some topics from this book, remember why you want to invest in cryptocurrencies (understand its philosophy), which platforms I can use to buy/store/trade bitcoin and altcoins, how to spot opportunities (with data from technical analysis and market study) and why blockchain/mining is important for us (as user and potential investor). But above all remember that you play the long term game, repeat your oath and have an investment strategy.

I wish you all good luck. My boss uses to say to me that good luck is for the unprepared, but in the cryptocurrency market and in this time stage (a lot of people claim that it is too early) we need all the necessary tools (knowledge, fate and luck).

www.ingramcontent.com/pod-product-compliance
Lightning Source LLC
Chambersburg PA
CBHW040058250526
45473CB00043B/1865